Scientific Papers

DAVID MORLEY was born in Blackpool and is of Romany extraction. He read Zoology at Bristol University, gained a fellowship from the Freshwater Biological Association in Windermere and pursued research on acid rain until the government closed the laboratory. He then travelled in Eastern Europe and reported on the revolutions of 1989. In 1996 he founded with Jeremy Treglown the Writing Programme in the Department of English and Comparative Literary Studies at the University of Warwick where he now develops and teaches new practices in scientific as well as creative writing. He has received a major Gregory Award, a Tyrone Guthrie Award from Northern Arts, a Hawthornden Fellowship, an Arts Council Writers Award, and an Arts Council Fellowship in Writing at Warwick University. His textual public artworks include collaborations with the sculptors/artists Francoise Schein, David Annand, Jochen Gerz, Kate Whiteford and David Ward. He has edited a new edition of *Jude the Obscure* for Könemann, and co-edited *The New Poetry* for Bloodaxe, a Poetry Book Society Special Commendation. In 2002 he edited *The Gift*, an anthology of new writing for the National Health Service, 30,000 copies of which were given to the NHS workforce. A handbook, *Under the Rainbow: Writers and Artists in Schools* is published by Bloodaxe/Northern Arts and was given to teachers in the North of England. His work has appeared in The British Council's *New Writing* and Faber's *Poetry Introduction* anthologies. *Scientific Papers* is the first section of a three-part sequence.

DAVID MORLEY

Scientific Papers

CARCANET

First published in 2002 by
Carcanet Press Limited
Alliance House
Cross Street
Manchester M2 7AQ

A CIP catalogue record for this book
is available from the British Library
ISBN 1 85754 567 2

The publisher acknowledges financial assistance
from the Arts Council of England

Set in Monotype Bembo by XL Publishing Services, Tiverton
Printed and bound in England by SRP Ltd, Exeter

For Siobhàn

intrai per lo cammino alto e silvestro
Inferno II

Acknowledgements

To the editors of the following publications where certain poems or versions of them were published: *Channel 4 Publications Rhyme and Reason, The Forward Book of Poetry 1993* and *2001, The Gregory Poems* (Hutchinson), *New Poetries III* (Carcanet), *New Writing 9* (Vintage), *Of Science* (Worple), *Poetry Introduction 7* (Faber and Faber); and also *Antigonish Review* (Canada), *Bête Noire, Exile* (Canada), *The Independent, London Magazine, The North, Oasis* (U.S.), *Oxford Poetry, PN Review, Poetry Review, Poetry Wales, Pretext, Prop, Quadrant* (Australia), *The Rialto, Salt* (Australia), *Scratch, Short Fuse: the Global Anthology of New Fusion Poetry* (edited by Todd Swift and Philip Norton, Rattapallax Press), *Stand* (New Series), *The Stony Thursday Book/Cuaderno de Madrid* (Spain), *The Tabla Book of New Verse 2001, Verse* and *The Wide Skirt*. Some of these poems were broadcast on Channel 4, BBC World Service, BBC Radio 2, BBC Radio 3, and CBC Radio Canada. Several pieces or drafts of them appeared in pamphlets and collections from Arc, Exile Editions (Canada), Prest Roots and Scratch.

Thank you to The Society of Authors Eric Gregory Trust; Hawthornden Castle International Retreat for Writers; Northern Arts and the Tyrone Guthrie Centre at Annaghmakerrig for a residency; The Arts Council of England for a Writer's Award; The Phoenix Trust for a number of public art commissions; The University of Warwick for an Arts Council Fellowship and, later, a Senior Fellowship during the period of writing. Belated gratitude to the Freshwater Biological Association for a Research Fellowship, and the School of Biological Sciences, Queen Mary Westfield; and to Sir Brian Follett, for helping me write my first scientific papers.

Contents

Scientific Papers

Darwin's compositional method is the serial development of signs. Bunches of examples. The selection of heterogeneous series. Putting functional examples at the centre of his argument. Imagine a scholar-gardener leading guests around his estate, stopping among the flowerbeds to offer explanations; or an amateur zoologist welcoming his good friends in a zoological garden. Here the demands of science correspond to one of the most fundamental aesthetic laws. I have in mind the law of heterogeneity which encourages the artist to seek to unite in one form the greatest number of different sounds, concepts of various origins, and even antithetical images.

Osip Mandelshtam, *On the Naturalists*, 1932

1

*An acceptable scientific paper must be the first disclosure
containing sufficient information to enable other people to do
three things: assess your observations, repeat your experiments,
and evaluate your intellectual processes. Your position has
everything to do with a system of reporting that is concise and
readily understandable. Each paper must be susceptible to
sensory perception and essentially permanent. Without
publication science is dead.*

What You Do and What You Say

A marine biologist, seaweed in my hair,
I have circled miles in this deep sea bell
waiting for its pressure to equal my blood,
feeling its strength when it arrives,

when the ocean floor stops swimming
and its film freezes, and oxygen
falls in you and your heart
from your mouth.

What you do, do it as though you meant it.
I have felt this as though I meant it:
circling a reef in the pilot ship, they say
Dive here. Begin looking.

I didn't come up at the end of my hour.
Like a lighthouse keeper I spiralled
the ocean's stairs, welled up to find the day
already turning.

Others more qualified stayed on the surface,
trained in the arts of oxygen and grapples.
The first of them to dive heard the language of coral,
bobbed up and sang bubbles in an inland bar.

The second to try it felt a tug on his air pipe
and swam up crying for the mother who held it.
The third was for sharks and a fourth stopped a sub
that split him like a mullet. The rest took to shore.

Hooked (they said), I was hooked. They said I was sent
on the bends in the decompression chamber.
What I did, said, that I was a born diver,
a porpoise, a scientist,

meant nothing to the boys in the engine room,
flat footed as walruses on their steel platforms,
who rounded one day and put the questions:
how deep was I diving? and in whose ocean?

When I dive, I do as seals, porpoises,
lampfish: let the fins rainbow
from my arms, gills from the ribcage.
What I say is how tides say it,

how the sea started us counting
as though we were meant to. What will you do? What
will you say when you are singing
under pressure as though you were meant to?

Bamboo

The way trees come out of their changing room in April
like green fighters, like players for a new season.
Or in the mathematics of that primrose, a perfect tense, and present.
The way the woodpigeon is inviolate yet
crashes like a child's plane through the oak canopy.

The way light on a forest floor serves as a prism
he can see only through his tempers and need.
As in crying the way his arms are folded up like wire wings;
how they make the shape of supplication, how they still mean *no*.
This bird is the shape and colour of his lie.

These are its wings and surrounding bamboo.
The knit of its weft and lattice is foolproof.
Its cage is a woodwormy pagoda with sliding splatter-tray.
And his lying tongue is the size of – *clasp it* – of a goldfinch.

And when all this is weighed and attended to and voiced
what can't be tempered by these few facts and codes?

I have lowered my voice while walking through this forest
not to capture something – *can you hear it moving?* –
but to eye-spy what vexes him so.
Is it the deer track treading blind into the road?

He waits behind and smokes himself slow.
It is five hours before he talks,
before silence runs from his mouth
like white chain, like smoke-rings: O – O.
Now listen to the bamboo rattling in his mouth.

Now sense the bird moving under his brow.
One second it might look out, its eye in his eye.
Now he will close his face and he will not be true.
For once he was.
And then the thing flew.

4

The Site

after Mandelshtam

Why am I trailing you,
now through a pine-wood, now
through the words I write,
going nowhere fast?

There's a gypsy encampment on the steppes,
newly moved in – sharp fires gone
by morning; the stamped ash
surrenders no clue or forwarding address.

I am in the pinewoods, trailing you.
There you were, like memory, a shackle.
Cling to me, you said.

Voronezh, January 1937

Gypsy Woman's Death

The carp of her tongue, the black shoal of gossip.
Her oath caught short by the district nurse's sly whisper.
Already the dogs slide like burglars beneath her trailer.
Fearing her, her daughters don't fear their husbands.
They will set fire to her caravan that evening.

§

Midnight or one he pads back to the caravan
and finds her gone, that scent sliding by the door.
He hears a nightjar then the sniggering river.
He breathes a hot cigar, burns the court order.
Midnight or one he flenses his breasts,
then rakes the blade over the wishbone of his legs.
His bond is his own, and the white bone.
The spaghetti about his wrist – more tubes and colours than telephone
                                                                cable.

It Requires Nothing

The last experiment needs no special equipment.
It won't take place in a laboratory or hospital.
Sterile or sullied surfaces: it doesn't matter.
You can remove those plastic gloves,
    that white coat.

Take off your clothes and feed them to the shredder.
Slip out of the catskin of your own skin now.
Remove personal belongings: spleen, heart, pancreas.
This is the final experiment. It requires nothing.
    Close your eyes.

Wasp

They found you cold, fists jammed on each other,
Arctic on Antarctica. And between them,
paper, scrawl: a crumpled note signed and sealed.
To release it meant prising a wrist,
cheating the knot of rigor mortis.
Then a policeman picked it with a jemmy…

Just once, this once, make sense of me?
Her words, questing, tightened their wire
across my chest. The car where they found you,
shut windows weeping with monoxide,
was hauled away; sold off to strangers
at a cut price they never fathomed.

Lies. All of it… a first, final readership,
hostaged to your death, in a coroner's office.
You should have shared. You didn't.
All this time… all that time, *you knew.*
Your parents bunched, stark as witnesses;
made for the door. You'd cut the ice.

§

Solstitial visitor, always the wasp
in your quick-fire combing along my shelves.
Were those books your pollen?
or the excuse for returning them
unread, spurning discussion
with a thrumming whisper, *bed?*
All reasons for talk squandered, unheard.
Only fear of love unsheathed your sting.

Quick – it's me. I unclenched the lock.
Snapdragon, campion: the flowerbed
no flower-bed, but a furnace of wasps
sizzling, dangerous. And you, waiting,
your shoes treading pollen,
gold-dust, haloes,
through brindled grass. And the trees
flexed over you like surgeons.

Ice. Our first winter: a glassy hive.
Honey in jars – bottles, sidelong,
whispered KILNER, KILN... KIL...
I dipped a spoon in the first of the year,
tugging the surface to a muscle of lava;
slipped it, neat, in your bowl of coffee.
Half-love, your love's language:
you stirred its black spiral.

Charred stubble in fields. The Winter's
burn-off snatched at your asthma:
a tantrum of breath
till I traced your inhaler.
That weekend, recovering, propped-up
with *Germinal*, you hauled one word
from your silted throat (*bed?*).
Winds outside made war on the aspen.

Snow. December; castanets of hail;
holly we brought in snared with hooks.
Taps betrayed us, a clanking mutiny
bursting a wall. We boiled snow:
snow on snow. Our windows, portholed
on a white atlantic, silently froze.
Bed, with the fire's dying collusion,
gave up its gift as we crammed for warmth.

§

Leaving unspoken what the doctor told you,
the clack of your step said: *Don't, don't,
don't*... I cut to the kitchen, jabbing
a kettle's thick, cool waist for coffee.
London in March. A second opinion
grudged the first. *Anything to be done?*
Nothing between us the train couldn't say,
hammering northward: *too late too late.*

Not now: your touchy, embattled cry
as I steered you from silence, hoping you'd walk
a little of the way. 'The woods perhaps?
a tree-creeper's nested.' But: *No – you
go*. I'd veer out, make eighty yards
before I stopped, stranded with wonder:
your seeping, last hours (minute by minute)
traduced to a bird on shrivelled bark.

That silence. I tried it.
An anchor scudding the sea-floor,
you were snared on a weightless sand;
for days you couldn't move or speak.
Then, a false Spring:
you asked for food; for your bed
to be placed in the hall-way
as though you'd fledge.

Your silence was fear, furled like a sting.
Your dad called by to run you to hospital.
Wants me to go and get it over!
You swayed to the car where your father
sat smoking. *Cunt – I'll die
where I like*

                    slamming to the bedroom,
snatching your things.

§

20

They found you cold, the car's drained engine
ticking to zero; you, flexed over yourself,
catapulted to that final wish: an Arctic quiet;
the sealight torching your eye like a mirror...
I came home to cupboards – their after-life, memory;
your clothes strewn about, burgled from wardrobes.
And the garden: its hive, a Vesuvius of larvae,
fresh tenants of this frozen site.

The Wasp

after Mandelshtam

I grow a wasp's eyesight behind my eyes.
It storms my head with needles.
I'm hurtling straight through sound
and remember everything:
all necessary detail, every move we made.
My head's on fire. I'm flying into colour
with only the slightest effort.
There's a flicker of yellow on my retina
the shape of Georgia. Inside that, a man
with mask, gloves, flail, swipes at a nest.
And it is the size of the earth.

Voronezh, February 1937

Oceanography

i

Apart from the sea we have the weather
in common, but the morning moves on
like a dunlin, precarious, stilt-walking
on her own reflection. A steamer's vapour
has collapsed on itself over the ocean.

Someone is dozing beneath the low planking
of the jetty. He knows that tomorrow
the mist will deepen, again it will snow,
the sky will come with something like hail.
Meanwhile, he has a worm-ridden bed
for sleep. Meanwhile, fishermen sling nets
from the rounded bay where a single sail
slows to a cloud. The nets come up empty.

ii

The grass is marram grass and the sand, sand.
These are facts that hang on everything.
Beyond the heath are meadows that send
entire crops to the big city. Everything hinges
on this; any sign of life is the weather breathing.

After the meadows and steppes, the Volga.
River, I thought I'd mislaid you like a mirror.
For days I didn't belong to your shoreline
until I drank you down, felt your sharp tongue
etch on my voice a clear voice of water.
No mention of your tide's slow censoring;
anything can happen, and everything.

Mathematics of Light

The wavelengths of daylight
register on bright equipment:

flutterings across a spectrum
from infra-red to ultraviolet.

Discover me at an ice age,
at a midnight of colour,

in a place where rainbows
unbind themselves completely.

But you stand in the noon.
Shadows are inventing themselves

over your quickening retina;
the day moves on to shade

when spires are like pen-strokes
in the heat haze … It's

like Newton's gold trances
as he skimmed slates on the sea,

like Einstein's chatter over tea,
borealis, wispy cigarettes. It's

down to the human to live it, take
it in. Keep my sunlight warm for me.

A Charm Offensive

Perplex me again with those images:
a lantern; a candle;
a moth wing on half-a-moth.
As if you knew the answer.

As if you, too, were scorched and strange
embedded in wax. As if you were again
striding out into the dark, a scuttle crooked in your arm;
your caravan's windows deadly with bright, sticky insects.

Yes to your belief in factual images for love:
comets issuing out of nothing, the banter
of asteroid-storms off Saturn, fire swollen
in the sun and Creation swerving in and out of itself.

This is the night. The hour before sleep
or the pretence of sleep. Not dawn
that charm offensive of light behind trees.

Clearing a Name

Spindrift across Stalmine, a place you won't know.
Reedbeds, gyp sites; flat Lancashire's Orinoco.

I watch a mistle-thrush on a blown telegraph wire,
leave my car by the dead elm above the river.

The camp is two caravans. The police have just left.
Two blu-tacked Court Orders this wind can't shift

or the rain read. A girl squatting with a carburettor
on her bare knees. Another, older, in a deck-chair

spoons Pot Noodle. Their dad with his pride, no joy,
wrestles over the yawning bonnet of a lorry.

Mam is out, knocking Blackpool's door
with her basket of tack, toddler dressed-down with care

for the rending detail: no shoes. I watch
the father unbend, fumble at the fire, splice a match

from a stray half-wicker, then I come down.
He lets a welcome wait in another time,

twists a roll-up, nods OK to his staring daughters.
Eyes me like fresh scrap fenced from a dealer,

half-sorted, half-known. Yes; he knew our family
'more for what they were' – Hop-girls, Iron-boys –

'but they married out, and there's the end of it.
Your muck's paid no muck of ours a visit.'

A thin smile: 'Except your dad,
he came with the nose of Concorde

on worksheets reeking of grease and swarfega,
bleating "an inch is now a bloody centimetre".

What's up with your schools? I'd say. Him – "This *is* school."
We squinnied blueprints as if they were braille.

Taught ourselves ground-up. A small conversion.
If your muck had stayed in family, if your gran

not gone nosing *gaujo* like they were the end-all.
Now you've had your end, fair do's. Get off pal,

you're not burnt up on fags or dodgy work.'

The ends, we want; the means are half the work:

something in his grip, under my sleeve like veins,
where hands lock together, become the same,

'Arctic on Antarctica' … *I need background.*
The uncle on my mother's side. 'Pulled from a pond.

The police were out for a man. Any taig or gyp.
Guns broke for a chicken-shoot. They found him face-up

and it fitted. They shot shite in a barrel.'
That B-road where Lancashire discharges its spoil.

Split mattresses. Paint tins. Grim stuff in carriers.
The sign No Dumping No Travellers.

I make my way back to the car, running
the hard keys from hand to hand then, turning,

pocket them. I do not move. It is not smart to show
(that plain car by the woods) how and where you go.

One uncle of mine went swimming. His name is snow,
or thaw, or mud. And you wouldn't know.

13

The Errand

I came to a place where buildings were going up;
biscuits of slate sat wrapped in twine.
Earth moved like sugar, boiling,
against the metal of a dumper.
A machine dropped, dropped its yellow snout
nuzzling at joists it was hammering in.
When I got to my father I would learn
the heat of that impact, how you might
light paper from the surface two hours on.
The air meanwhile would shiver with fire,
a fineless dust, the shouts of impact.

He was with the welders –
a short-term hire – cutting thin plate
to microns. Not visored, he
stood out from that coven
of kneeled and sparking men
like something they were making
or melting to start over.
We went out to sandpiles, pounded stone,
his eyes spindling, his mouth
asking and asking why I was there.

Moonlighter

He might be my brother for all he is gyp.
His is not the time for pullovers and combs;
his plum shirt is Blackpool, very Blackpool.
I have watched his van for hours, from Marton Estate
to this traveller site; a mole in mole's clothing.
He will scrabble through the mud of everything:
the nuts and nuggets of marriage, a bolt of a ring,
weights of children, slack pulleys of police.
Burglar by night, a rain-soaked genius
of the jerry-built coastal pre-fab,
he stacks his van with valuables:
a deadman, a handspike, a parbuckle.
Lightning moves its show across the camp.

Σ

Our family eats the funeral sandwiches: pink paste and white bread.
My four saucy uncles pinch at their bits of tobacco.
They fall, clawing at fake heart attacks each time I come up to them.

We are in the kitchen of my dead grandmother's maisonette.
Her sisters squawk about compensation, weather, and the Third Eye.
One of my aunts goes spare: 'What's dead is dead.
We're small people. We can't take on the whole bloody NHS.'

The internal pressure burst the capillaries beneath my gran's eye
diagonally, like a whip might, opening her hale cheekbone up.
Sigma is the shape carved on that seventy-year-old face
where the care-worker screwed his fist around her nose to smash it.

The Wakes

On the blue, four and two.
On the white, your camera-light.
Blackpool queues, how do you do's.
Blackpool's wealth, the brain's on a shelf.
Knock it back. Bring it up.

Glasgow Wake. Run on the clubs.
The zoo on Sunday, its all-hour pub.
The girls of wire, their tiny men,
the kiss, the rub, the bye bye hymen.
Gold rushed in from the offshore rigs.
The black stuff, cash; the men, the cogs.
Barnsley Wake. The smuts of air,
the skinned-up blow, the Solacare.
Downwind of the weather cock –
Heysham trawlers, Fleetwood Macs,
the Cod War punching at their backs.
The Cod War, the coldest war.
Welsh Wake. The train's a throat
boozing through Preston, cacking through Kirkham,
spuming in the forth of Blackpool North.
The cut-throat cabs, the pugs, the blabs,
the shot up cases, the bastard scabs.
Blackpool queues, the threats, the bruise.
Miner's Wake. Had it good,
then Miners' Strike; Cortonwood.
The Miners' strike, then the English knife.
A policemen's lot: nasty, short.
Blackpool taunts, how do you don'ts.
Blackpool's wealth, the brain's on a shelf.
Irish Wake. Gypsy-speak –
Irish Stew in the name of the bore.
God rushed in to the Belfast yards,
an Irish Card, a prod old guard.
Then the dollar's breath, a year-long death;
a boom, a bust. The shipyard's rust.
Rochdale Wake. Drink till you choke.
Knock it back, dog it up.

Knock her up. Kiss her quick.
Dog her quick. Knock her back.
The North Pier and tackled up.
A haul of fish, the flask. The mug.

Clickety-click, full house, drop-kick.
Blackpool queues, how do you do's.
Blackpool's wealth, the brain's on a shelf.
On the blue, four and two.
On the white, your camera-light.

Nature of Memory

It flatters you with its ballet-stretch at the mirror,
a river of trained movements, its yawn and shiver –
waiting for you to call it into the world.
But above all, it flatters you.

Your brain is a sea. A memory
buoys, a private prodigality:
a red, laden ship in a limestone harbour,
dredgers drag its beaten shore.

Difficult, a memory is clearly sorrow.
It lies to you like your cornered boy
holding out his colourful plan
for an imaginary land built by him and for him.

Friendly and Equitable Insurance

I've been out in the woods and brought something home.
A creature, no, nor lichen sleeved from a branch.
I've been digging, not to lay a ghost
or to find a father, but to uncover the taproot
of that famous tree from the book of memory.
I post myself a report on its territory:
a nervous system of root, the brain of leaf,
perennial synapses of forgettings and rememberings.
And when I receive it I will not believe in it;
bin it with my father and all the creatures,
dead or imagined, not worth the risk,
a risk that could make me hate myself.

The next morning I will not go to the woods.
I'll read about my death by easy payments.
For if my eyelash offends I pluck it.
If the city grows too hot I leave it,
hitting the countryside with its big-hearted hedges,
vistas and many sites of historical interest.
In everything I do, I offend something.
The taproot oozes oil, spreads across my memory,
blacks and confuses it. I must do as I please
with this sunlit morning: the light is accurate
and I stand square as though I owned it.
As though I deserved it no more.

The Spectra

after Mandelshtam

I have come for you and I have seen you.
It is a miracle. For once, you're going nowhere,
neither out to walk the rounds of the horizon
nor home to scribble white lines about it.

I half see you through that knife-hole in the ice,
past shivering, staring back. Have you stopped here forever,
the record of your death still spinning,
that snow death you always longed for?

It is like this, my love, where skaters
swerve beyond you, where the horizon's lightning
makes you run any place but towards it:
it is like nothing on earth.
The sun is seven pure fires
and they in turn will come for you.

Voronezh, January, 1937

Like Coral

He looked up, and realised he was blind.
Where was the lake? More to the point
who was the character yanking at his hand?
The voice behind it had a familiar accent

and the words, well, the words were something;
they were simple, limpid, sweet as oil.
He couldn't get enough. He was still listening
as the words hardened around him like coral.

But the blindness, how could he explain that?
If it were to finish by waking up, how his public
would laugh at him! Perhaps he should shout.
Perhaps he should address his questions to the lake

but that would be careless. Whoever the bastard
was he could certainly talk. And it was worth
listening to. It was like hearing the world.
Or like the way seabirds are tuned into the surf's

white noise despite the distance and land-mass.
Maybe he was being offered a sound-map, a system
if you like, for all the necessary answers
his interrogators would prise from him.

★

The castle windows are as big as doors. Outside
five cars have tremored to a halt, their engines
smoking with cold. They are black and wide
and official. The snow clutches the perfect lines

of their wheels. Soon, there will be foot-prints
ghosting the courtyard, shouts, lamplight.
Something, say a fox, might look from a distance.
A bird, say a nightjar, might disturb the quiet

for a second. There is more to it than snow
stroking the roof. More to it than marksmen
posted on the main gates. But somebody departs on cue,
running softly through the half-invisible gardens.

*

Hard going, with snow covering him like fur.
When he reached the lake, touched down
on water, he felt where his shoulder –
well, where it ached, where the razor had been,

where a quick red cut was opening and closing
like a mouth. *Priorities. Keep them in mind.*
Priority one. Control the shivering.
Priority two. Hide, hide from the wind.

Quoting Yourself

I have friends who do this.
Kneel to a mirror and whisper
while the audience before them
is silent as the reflection of the room.

How the mirror would like to eat their faces! –
gulp and digest as if they were Alice.
I grip the phone, punch their numbers.
Each of them, gone. I have friends who do this.

Nobody wants children anymore.
We quote our children out of the air.

The Goodnight

An owl unfolds across the bed:
its eyes, hungover can see the dead;
the swerving and the narrow hours
are no longer mine, no longer yours:
perfect ships of life and work
butt each other in the dark.

While adulterers in their box-rooms stuff
straw into their whinnying love,
and swimmers-out-of-sight clear
the deep-water and the disappear,
dreamers in their tents will know
that snow will light the night for now.

Light we taught to obey our touch
is surrendered to the switch.
The asthma of our deaths goes deep.
We are not alive in sleep:
the panic of my child at night
is the world's unbearable flight.

23

Posterity

Mande will sollohaul neither bango nor tatcho
'I swear now neither falsely nor truly'
Romany law

i Cast

Cars silting at the lights, the river of a bypass,
some Long Vehicle skidding like slate-slaps on water.
There are wormcasts in the way: protesters dug in –
ground-nesting, broody, flappy with media attention.
The rain curls back, European and guilty.
It air-drops news at a horrible tilt.
Stop now, with no more effect than you stop.

ii Buying satsumas for my son

I look down and I see my son.
I am buying satsumas for him.
He feels my fingers close against his own.
He holds one arm up, half-surrendering.
He feels my fingers close against his own.
The clench and tang: the citrus-tongue unwinding.
He holds one arm up, half-surrendering
something he wants, but what, he can't yet say.
The clench and tang – that citrus-tongue unwinding
in his palm now, like the unwinding of a gift:
something he wants, but what he can't yet say
and he is barely breathing, holding it all
in his palm now. Like the unwinding of a gift
he uncurls his hand from mine
and he is barely breathing, holding it all.

'The audience claps – we know it is our families
out there with witnesses;
their watches time our exit.
We go a month of Mondays,
rushing for toast, car keys
that exist only when they feel like it.

We stuff ourselves in the habitat called everybody.
Of course you must have the car
and I must have the baby.
A blackbird performed from a tree.
An audience of two starved of applause.
Both our windows were wide.'

iv   Woken early Sunday morning

It was the dream again, the drum, not Isaac
crying early in his night-travelling cradle:

*I am the voice of your murder, your very own
cabbage-white, afloat on electricity,
your impossible unmanned flight,
the Atlantic, the tide's static, white noise
of your brain's knowing and forgetting; the kite
that climbs ten ladders of wind, and snake-dives
its fifty-butterflied tail ...*
                    Dear dead,
the voice is possibly your own,
that place you call from, that habit of not breathing –
impossible, an art:
a science unmade from the human.

'In the lightbulb over your desk,
one of those "chaos-butterflies"
startles some minor ink-storm
off the coast of her page,
a marginal note.
Like a petal it opens: *he loves me not.*

I've lost our thread
and, with it, literally, my head.
That head: held in hands head,
Gallipoli-shot-going-over-the-top head,
stormcloud and lightning-hair head.

Ocean-going, the heart – a liner,
from my eyes' breached portholes to the heart's hank.
I smoke, and lifeboats respond to each stalled flare
feathering into search-teams (each her face).

She, reading the back of the hand of the sea.'

vi   Pollen

His eyes are on tulip-stalks
because of that kid's bike
our next-door-widow delivers up
from the back of her husband's den.
The thing embarrasses her.
Ten years in hiding, it's like new.
My son and I race it through her orchard.
I'm on my knees straddling the machine
when he goes crazy –
                or his *hands* go
wrenching, ripping, every apple blossom in reach.
I pulled at the wreckage. Plates or confetti.

Smashed, I typed, I will not die, on a computer screen.

'Here is the scallop ashtray you will throw at me.
That grey ashy crap could be cigarettes or lava,
my own sputum or your tiny ashmound answers,
your *no* and *no* and *no*
(you go it at the mirror)
go on and on and on.

It's dawn and the coffee-chorus.
We're as embarrassed as mirrors.
I unfold the map, and where to meet.
You unfold the out-of-court, and out-of-my-sight.
Brinkmen, we take our breaths away.
Pull a mirror to our lips. Alive.'

viii   Posterity

I have danced in my son's heart – its corridors.
I will dance. I push fruit into his palms and dance.
An orchestra tunes up. The music swarms.
Now we will taste the winter's colours.

And my child will sit under a green tree
and in my heart like hot snow.
And who will tug him from his name and skin.

Osip Mandelshtam on the Nature of Ice

1933

i

I'd read about glaciers and I'd seen glaciers. How a stream runs
under their bellies, sluices from their lower reaches. What it fetches
up along the way: the whole sides of mountain, gripped and ground through
its kidneys. And the taste of it as water, both sweet and sullied
or tender as blown glass. Which explains how in poems I confuse
glaciers and glaziers. Which won't explain why I am becoming
both ice and glass.

ii

He's forgetting when it started but during his exile years
they never owned a mirror. The sheen on ice supplied something
of the sort. On washing day – what little they had got bashed and
rinsed in a sink in a local theatre – he'd finger out a small
ice-mirror from a puddle, walk with Nadezhda to that grimy
theatre. And they were suddenly respectable to themselves,
staring into its tiny rink. While it lasted.

iii

How to stop ice melting from contact with live hands? Or being
flashed to crystal by every movement? I learned this on placement
in the Petersburg factories: a trick used by glaziers: slip
plate-glass in silk and, between forefinger and thumb,
gently pinch the opposing ends. It gives birth to a
pressure: it tensions lines of force which are
hurtling through the mass like waves.

iv

The secret was this: with each move he made, he
made his body ride on that new born force-field. Like
carrying a child: like walking on water: vigorously,
tenderly, he strode as if he were ice.

v

The charm was in the looking:
I became frozen to my image. Out of earth, out of water,
I ran clutching the ice-mirror. Through forests,
through rain. But all I know is: I
would wake walking, in controlled
free-fall, diamonds
in my fist.

Two Temperatures for Snow

As if the snow itself were a country
with pleasure gardens, hotels, religion,
babyware, and the word yes and the word no.

You enter its capital along the paths of slush.
Signs direct you to the City Elder. Nothing will grow
under her rule, as Signs will tell you at every corner.

But when she invites you to her Ice Festival
you will learn to love Slowfreeze and Nightflake,
her daughters by sunless adoption. Will they dance,

dance with you? Only so slowly unless they melt
at the heart from a heat of ecstasy. The parquet
is white, white. You are falling out of life.

Their images are locked in you forever.
You will carry them, bright on your lips,
even over oceans, to your own easy gardens.

One night you may wake before dawn,
walk naked to where the river thaws
in its grave. Beneath a bridge of smoothest limestone

put your ear against the ear of winter
listening for a yes, a no. Or touch
where the words enter the water,

ii

and do none of these things. Call at the office.
When someone says yes the answer is no.
File your dockets in bin bags for burning

the moment when a stranger rides up in the elevator.
Meanwhile, talk of weather or the terrible storm damage.
Avoid words like informer, auditor, police.

There are things in the wall very like ears.
Their microphones are wonderful as knots in wood.
Listen, someone can sell you at the slightest notice

with a single nod. So they will come for you
in the small hours. To snout through your past
rabid for evidence. To ask you to repeat after them,

yes, yes, yes. Through it all they will help with heat
to the arms, chest, your white lips. Then, peace,
a dream of snow, cold hands holding you,

which you love; that lift you to where water
rushes over your face. Will you dance, dance?
Only so slowly. Melting, melting.

47

Two Haiku Pennants

after Einstein, after Minkowski

$$x'^2_1$$

$$+$$

$$x'^2_2$$

$$+$$

$$x'^2_3$$

$$x^2_1$$

$$+$$

$$x^2_2$$

$$+$$

$$x^2_3$$

Fulcrum/Writing a World

'While I talk and the flies buzz,
a seagull catches a fish at the mouth of the Amazon,
a tree falls in the Adirondack wilderness,
a man sneezes in Germany,
a horse dies in Tattany, and twins are born in France.
What does that mean? Does the contemporaneity
of these events with one another,
and with a million others as disjointed,
form a rational bond between them,
and write them into anything
that resembles for us a world?'

Special and General Theory

Of characters *X* and *Y* in a box with their friends,
their closed society.
Of an alleyway
where the traffic – that film – of history has to roll.
That's where a box is upending itself constantly.
It propels itself down the streets of Tenochtitlan
as though it contained some important message
or the wind was blowing it with some plan in mind.
Of an imago hatching on Montezuma's open squares.
Of the beginning of the beginning of a long sleep.
Of Montezuma coloured with the paints of sacrifice.
Of the citizenry's neglect of animal husbandry
a toast to the gods in their bloodbath.
The land is as dry as you would expect with a land of this name
whose name is not spoken until the rains broach it.
The box does not stop the people in their labours;
the guts of many cows are in the hands of the multitude,
the necks of dark birds, all their superfluity.
The box isn't watched at all – it becomes like Captain Cook,
and his ship those aborigines couldn't perceive as true.
It just rocks down the street where children
watch its progress with peculiar attention.
They are waiting for it to stop. They want to probe the interior,
if it contains the famous Emperor Moths of the Aztec Empire.
Of the children who prize them, but a priest commands them to prize them.
Such moths are our gods, they have taken the colours of fire,
they are our birthday selves, they share our blood.
In an alleyway in a pre-Hispanic city, the movement of the box
must be the movement of ten thousand wings.
Something mountainous reaches into a pocket for the sun
and the scene is lit, the long path of the volcano is super-visible.
You must taste the skin of a volcano while this story lasts.
The story won't be sustained, it will go off like a horse from gunshot
taking with it characters X and Y.
It will marry them. It will turn them into conventional narratives,
and that figure like a father-figure is not a visual joke,
but an image of the box that has rocked up there
like a walker beleaguered by mosquitoes.
There is a graph accompanying this. It is on the overhead projector

and the screen is bigger than both of us, up there on the skyline.
Information lopes across in its motley
of sea breezes and mountain breezes. The hare at the foot
of the graph demands correlates, grass and flea powder.
Somebody draws a line. Somebody an equation.
The slope fits the hillside.
You find yourself in the landscape, in this time zone, or in the box.
You want to live, you want to get out of the box.
But the stony tops of volcanoes are troublesome,
are volatile. They are like tall things in childhood
when tallness is terrifying.
The box becomes something to you. You begin to value its progress.
You want to throw water at its fire. You want
to turn it off, the dangerous switch.
You make your way through the streets of Tenochtìtlan.
You'd like Cortez to arrive with ten thousand men.
That would be useful,
water and men are usually useful at some juncture.
But they haven't been born. Spain is still frictioning off
the land-plates of Africa.
You remember, most of the world
is still ablaze –

The graph changes with your movements, it becomes a parabola.
It seems to fall away with your mood. You must watch yourself.
You must be confident, make footprints and gestures that show this.
The citizenry will elect you Elector, the graph grow exponential.
That would be something, there will be plenty of fat, sleek princelings.
There will be a beguiling of cultivation to supply their bellies.
You want to live, you want the answers now.
How the priests had something on their minds, chucking the seedcorn.
How the donkeys were resting,
foreseeing a demand for religions.
How things build up to things, build down.
Your whole spine drops out of your back and snakes off to copulate.
You want it back, you don't want this kind of separation!
You propel yourself down the streets searching for a prop-up.
It comes into your hands in the form of a long bow,
a scimitar, a claymore, a Kalashnikov.
Of your history that tears you to pieces in limbfuls.
Of your not being able to get away with anything.
So you want the graph to have you on it? –
go on
you can use my pen.

Albert Einstein in America

1933

i

Light is flung out of the State.
    It understands us, how our place is set.
        Escape through it.

ii

Glass heart, bone-strung feather,
    the light shapes a mirage from our sweet share.
        Escape through its weather.

iii

How the birds of sorrow
    have eaten out the heart of this running light.
        Escape through tomorrow.

iv

A cloud rows air above the groves
    then tacks in a breeze beyond cypresses.
        Escape in their clothes.

v

Escape through their dead,
    through their teeth, bones, their vivid cramped arms.
        It is time.

In a Winter Palace

Kerensky makes a fist
around the last bottle
still florid with claret.
He has failed; and fails

to feel his arousal
at the naked thought
of women, lithe
on porcelain.

This night he rips his mouth
prising the neck
of the Tsar's *Yquem*
baring only his teeth.

How his lips stretch
at the memory of wine!
He laps the brown foreskin
of a *marron glacée.*

But now, in his element,
the Tsar's coarse ghost
follows him everywhere
with a hand-held camera,

an eye on the light-meter
— *Were those my shadows?* —
that two-way mirror
his glimmering pince-nez …

But why that special look
towards the library floor
where a map of Russia
rolls shorter each hour?

And the immense Reading Room
prepared as though for a banquet
with Tolstoy as *entrée*?
He fondles a complete set

of Chekhov, a *demi-monde*
of dark-bound Dostoyevsky.
Kerensky breaks the bind
of the Tsar's desk diary,

his fashion-conscious index
of silky dead mistresses.
An exquisite marginal note,
His final edict.

An earlier order (scrawled)
for Safe Passage. And another
(to the Imperial Apothecary)
for Spanish Fly.

The Field–note

after Mandelshtam

Warships are breaking the ice-canals
but their bows are braced
against something
which isn't real.

There's a trail of oil spidering from the hulls.
Women and sailors stare
from the pier
where the water

booms from fantastic pumps. It says:
They wait here forever because they were never here.
The wind goes on waxing
a seagull's moustache of offal.

Voronezh, December, 1936

Ozymandias to You

A poet stayed a month in my half made building:
a trellis of iron, my hopeless skyscraper-to-be.
    The poet liked girders, said they were line endings.
He said they were the line endings of Vladimir Mayakovsky.
    He took the room above the liftshaft and he loved the echoes,
        echoes were second nature.

I told him of my cement mixers, two years in coming
and look, damn it, at all this Industrial Sand.
    He said, useless, Egyptian, and went about in shorts.
It was a murderous summer, he said,
    a crucial time to be planning any restructuring
        or poems in couplets.

Leave it to Nature, he said. I did. I hopped it
and left the building site open to the weather.
    One big storm and my site became Sudan,
an overnight fairground for all the local children.
    They had never seen my sea, the tide was always out
        somewhere, out there.

The tide was always out and the sands were of my making.
Oh, employees lorried in from satellite villages!
    How you picnicked with vodka, your wives and girls,
hatched natterjacks under my corrugated iron,
    belched incorrigibly, made love by the brick piles.
        Roman love, the real thing.

They liked me for allowing it and came to me singing.
I was suddenly famous for all the wrong reasons.
    All the wrong reasons were rightly too tempting.
The poet wrote my eulogy or was it an elegy?
    He lifted it from the *Collected* of Percy Bysshe Shelley,
        a Party Man apparently.

He said their folksy traditions and late night stories
were resurrecting in the sands. My sands, I mean.
   Well, there was certainly something: madrigals, rhapsodies.
There were certainly candles, all night blow-outs,
   the colossal wreck of bonfires in the morning,
      their strange, charred hearts.

When the police finally raided I hoiked up a megaphone.
They thought it was a blunderbuss, lobbed the CS gas in.
   The poet caught it in the face but was lucky;
it was just one of his many masks, the one marked *Posterity*.
   He made shift with ten other masks he threw to the children
      with appropriate instructions.

He said the Architecture of Realism was a fixed route up Vesuvius.
That the police were the sherpas, the coolies, the carriers.
   Our position in Time was sufficient to justify,
well, expeditions into anything, if it led to lucidity.
   He said he would write us up (this was above our heads)
      by charring every word.

He said other things beside, not all of them clear.
We took up with the singing though there wasn't any choice.
   So I showed them the blueprint the moment we were finishing
and tore it before them and h a n d e d it to the police.
   We took a while to vanish, but the process was starting
      from the first white tear

and continued ▓▓▓▓▓▓▓▓▓▓▓▓▓▓▓▓▓▓▓▓▓▓▓▓▓s
▓▓▓▓▓▓▓▓▓▓▓▓▓▓▓▓▓▓▓▓▓▓▓▓▓ through history
▓▓▓▓▓▓▓▓▓▓▓▓▓▓▓▓▓▓h until a smear of snow ▓▓▓
▓▓▓▓▓▓ like a slick of ▓▓▓▓▓▓▓▓▓▓▓▓▓▓▓▓▓▓
▓▓▓▓▓▓▓▓▓▓▓▓▓▓▓o! semen was all that
      remained of us.

The Aftermath

after Mandelshtam

'The dawn-trees float their dark coral
as though a sea had left them standing:
      they testify to the visible
      temerity of creation.'

'Then who has been here before us?
Who wrote us in the mist? painted our
      images into morning, as though
      we owned the faces of children?'

'It isn't always winter here:
the small fields are shaping themselves
      through the thaw. I would count on so much.'
      But the trees are a dark coral.

Voronezh, February 1937

Darwinian

An invasion mechanism: the fish sift the water.
They ingest the right particles, also the wrong.
Bacteria implode under the stomach's pressure.
Surviving microbes migrate to dorsal flesh.

Two freshwater biologists in a smack, upstream.
An hypothesis as thin as the paper they wrote it on.
Tears at bedtime for fish with the bacterium-strain.
Their eyes, pustular. Their considerations, air.

A boat, humped over, in the littoral of a river.
A beetle heading – where – across its bow.
Science at midnight on the far edge of a lake.
Our best work carried out on the shore of sleep.

The observations: tiny, as essential as daybreak:
a reedbed rowing its sundial out of sync;
a spider hauling dead up in rainbows;
and Saprolegnia, a parasite of fish.

I turned into a fish one morning and drowned.
Fish-hearted at The Benefit, I had lost my face.
How I swam into unemployment. How my girl's face knew.
In Parasite Science, no place for this knowledge.

The humane director of the freshwater laboratory.
He was 'released from employment' with one week's notice.
His final task was to sack all his staff.
I met him twice afterwards. We had lost our faces.

He lost himself in a gardener's job.
The Park's Department had a place for his knowledge.
Someone, somewhere has place for our knowledge.
The local park had the place for his knowledge.

Christ calls from the kitchen. We make lunch together.
Fish. Let's grill them, but we strip off their skin.
We flense off the parasites, wait for the five thousand.
Then I wrap him in white lines like a Bird Eating Spider.

Intexti

I have studied the science of saying goodbye
Mandelshtam, 'Tristia'

Immarcescible knowledge of a dumped girl
sends short-circuits through the author, as below:

'In Poe's Valentine poem to Frances Sargent Osgood
she finds her name spelled by the first letters of the line.'

'In the phrase-net Jesus-Christ-God's-Son-Saviour
shivers the Greek noun for fish: *Icthys*.'

'In Alexandria and in the Middle Ages, the pattern-poems
scripted by such as Boniface, Bede, Fortunatus.'

'In the East, the ring-poems' – I would saltmarch the stanzas;
'similarly the mushrooming Japanse kakushidai.'

You mean you temper your insignificant sorrows, my friend asks,
shaping verses that meet the laws of a microcircuit?

'I cannot bear the thought of her sleeping with him.'
Sleeping? She will not be – wags forefingers – *'sleeping'*.

I think you should get out more. Forget her.
Slip some girl a length of the old etcetera.

Isn't art's job to hack hard sonnets from the loved? –
something like the 'Amorosa Visione', like thrice-balled Boccaccio?

In that phrase I love you (what is is no more),
simultaneous combustion of former girl's letters, who he loved.

A Conception

It is dawn when they lift each other upstairs.
There are wounds in the carpet where their bed goes mad.
That day the ice is shaken from the eaves.
Something is gathered, and is gathering a name.

There are wounds in the carpet where their bed goes mad
tottering on daft feet and dancing down the room.
Something is gathered, and is gathering a name:
it wants to lift itself, he or she, at once to go
tottering on daft feet and dancing down the room
with its own life and limb. And the lovers know this.
It wants to lift itself, he or she, at once to go
at their speed in its own conception from these two
with its own life and limb. The lovers know this;
stripped, in new reticence, they listen to it sing
at their speed, in its own conception, and from these two.

They wake each other with their movements. It's Christmas night.
Stripped, in new reticence, they listen to it sing.
(That day the ice was shaken from the eaves.)
They wake each other with their movements. It's Christmas night
and dawn when they lift each other upstairs.

Redwings and Magnetism

How small is the god of those migrating bird-rivers:
redwings, fieldfares that fall from Norway to the Neva.

She will climb from her bed and airbrush their science.
The season is ice-mist, a scared short-range weather.

Redwings, fieldfares that fall from Norway to the Neva
smash as if thrown against the solid-state river.

The season is ice-mist, a scared short-range weather.
A small neck bows, the tiles of its wings

smash as if thrown against the solid-state river.
She makes herself dark coffee, taps in the data.

Her small neck bows; the tiles of those wings
are unfolded and healed by the heat of her argument.

She makes herself dark coffee, taps in the data.
How those ten thousand birds fleer in her thought,

unfolded and healed by the heat of her argument.
Warm the cold lives by her limpid knowledge:

those ten thousand birds that fleer in her thought.
She has climbed from her bed, airbrushed their science,

warmed the cold lives by a limpid knowledge:
how small is the god of those migrating bird-rivers.

'Hawk Roosting' Revisited

Predation-strategies 'rehearsed',
i.e. activity diurnal, predatory;
Rapid Eye Movement when dormant.

Hierarchical niche-structure, theoretically.
Habitat when inactive: forest canopy.
Predation strategies 'rehearsed', i.e.

100% attentive to prey stimuli;
proactive at a feeding opportunity.
Rapid Eye Movement when dormant.

Function of cognition: prey quality.
Perceptual limitations during inactivity.
Predation strategies 'rehearsed', i.e.

moves over identical zone in territory.
Male: dominant, sexually.
Rapid Eye Movement when dormant.

Highly-pressured, environmentally.
Future absence from food web: probably.
Predation strategies 'rehearsed', i.e.
Rapid Eye Movement when dormant.

The Motion of Deer

Killing a Doe

The deer come running, running –
a shock of things

that are not deer;
they clump and churn like tractor wheels,
crap out their fear: *run*.

A tattered move; one is all
it takes to flick one down:

a hind that casts her footing
slaps the ground, runs
the radius of a cracked leg;

this is not birth, the getting-up
on legs, but close, close.

§

A stone takes all the hand, for stone
wants to be down at speed

or quickly placed. It requires
knack to get it right –
to split the difference

between the stone's falling,
and a precise cranial bone
of a panicky deer
but this is how it runs.

§

This is how deer run. There is no mystery.
The leading hoof scouts forward

in a search for levels,
the tailing three make do
with taken ground.

Sometimes the earth prepares
mistakes: maze-sphagnum, pot-holes...
so brakes are slammed on every hoof,
the cleats close up like scared anemone;

there is no cease but
grace-notes in the running.

In a Deer's Eye

The deer come running, running –
    a shock of things which are not deer –
        they

clump and churn like tractor wheels –
    crap out their fear –
        run.

There is no cease
    but a tattered move:
        one is all it takes.

The tailing three make do
    with taken ground – this
        is how it runs this

is how deer run: close, close –
    to get it right,
        grace notes in their running...

A hind that casts her footing
    slaps the ground,
        runs the radius of a cracked leg;

the leading hoof scouts forward
    searching levels –
        maze-sphagnum, pot-holes.

A panicky deer takes all the hand for stone,
          wants to be
             down at speed or –

quickly brakes are slammed on every hoof,
          the cleats close up –
             scared anemone.

Sometimes the earth mistakes, prepares.
          This is not birth,
             the getting-up on legs, but

split the difference between falling
          and precise cranial bone,
there is no mystery.

Air Street

Deer tracks – I followed them: made
a forest slide through a deer's eye; felt

for myself the trodden dints of hoof,
their short codes cut in the frost.

But pitch of night: the running shrews
seethe like short-circuits on the wet leaf-base.

My torchbeam welds them to the ground.
I could gather them like moss.

The air as well, abrupt with movements
walks with me like gravity

and, step by step, it flenses sound
to whispers of a deer-cut.

Where the tracks street together
like passes of a scalpel

with torchlight off, eyes wide for catlight,
I smelled their musks like creosote

and saw the deer – a herd of ten –
scent me there and go.

Morning took me south, levelled on fat
curving rails, restive station platforms,

ticks of rain on the hard glass.
As if trespassing I cut the close-wire of people.

Gundogs grabbed me at traffic lights.
Gamekeepers in Downing Street

met my stare.
It was night delivered me this:

another street lit by nothing
and then the name like nothing: AIR.

The Transition

after Mandelshtam

What's left of the morning is probably good:
milk, tea, black bread, the minutiae of exile.
  But what we are told in this ordered room
    won't please the escort or the gods.

They've given me four years to survive my name.
(The landlord calls me everything under the sun.)
  What's left of the morning is probably good
    but it doesn't please the escort or the gods.

A farmer came today, gave us oats and kale
to make good broth, to see us through the worst.
  The escort eats his fill, goes back to bed.
    (What's left of the morning is probably good.)

So, we walk to a hill where legend has it
a boy lived with a peacock. He was thought a god.
  He fed on rainbows, scarlet milk. He *was* a god.
    It pleased everyone to think so. And they survived.

Now he's wrapped underground with all he had.
His body's his own, was it also theirs?
  They'd picked him over, found he wasn't a god
    but all too human, all too dead.

What's remembered of him can't be bad.
I like the way they buried him with seeds.
  The escort shouts us back. He thinks he's god.
    What's left of the morning is probably his.

Voronezh, December, 1936

42

Mermaid

The newspapers in the library will tell all you wanted.
How a man was listening as the fogs scrolled ashore.
You will start to hear the tale as though the sound
were a woman actually lilting and not a siren.

What is the truth? Why did he burst the door?
and what was that he was mewling, shouting?
'It was neurosis, no, but her voice came swimming.'
She was a pillage of fish stinking his bed out.

She was dragged from the harbour, watched by children.
She was probed by a forensic team down from Fleetwood.
She was a woman but *it* was not a woman.
It was taken to a shipping lane and slid overboard.

In the Fishery HQ, Doctors Z____ and R_____
were slow to bring up the arterial brightness
of the wound, which they saw, or they said they saw,
and her fishtail sliced and cut like a dress.

It was behavioural psychosis. It was nothing more.
It was the drag of the nets at the end of a pier.
It was a bad case of passion. The broken law.
It was a sea-lane to nowhere and somebody saw.

Rodin's Physics

Smoke withers into life. It flows to an opacity
and its deft stone is cut from the sharpest energies

in fire: a compliance, a pliant slate of smoke,
a broken form turned blunt-end to the ground.

Stoking up, you flesh that sparse contracted source.
The flame-points swell with wings and cobbled smoke.

Masking a fist, you weave in half-burnt oak
and stand away, watching how the falling-up of heat

quarries the air of flakes and its finity.

A sculptor works less openly,
releasing stone in secret,

scraping out caves to find their captive,
hands like drills. The binds of stone

shrivel to his touch: a plying flame
as if fumbled out of smoke.

He makes his fist a phoenix:
hands he turns are wings that clench a fire;

a beak that bites is a chisel in this stone.
The warm wings lift a trembling limb from rock.

Live dust, like smoke, veers into air.

The New Life

after Mandelshtam: after Dante

i

As with autumn, so with spring,
both tedious leave taking,

ice chinking in the gutters,
the river's ridiculous swagger.

We moved like that once,
our minds thawing with bottle after bottle.

I would sing like Dante, exhausted
by the night before, the night to come.

Say I'm the ghost of what I am.
I watched a log-pile turn into a village

with the first ember of morning.
Nobody has to tell me it's illusion.

ii

Low pressure over Voronezh.
The barometer held its breath.

I'm foot-slogging snow drifts
at the edge of the world.

It's a virtual white-out.
Where the paths end up is nobody's business.

Nor where I end up, head down in the water, listening to vast forests grow.

Voronezh, January 1937

Simultaneity

All this is happening

i

Avenues. Lawns. Parterres.
Lanterns in all the known trees.
The courtly insurrections
of light and dark –
all this is happening
in a new Siberia,
in the white cities
below the snowline.
The cities recline
in a pragmatic circle
from which the labour camps
are barely visible.

ii

One river runs to the cities
(its sources are scattered
and cannot be traced).
This river is a necklace
of tributary streams
which are swollen each day
by a trance
of bloodless sunlight;
an ocean once covered
this entire continent.
No prisoner will forgive
the mist which conceals him.

iii

The city pavements glimmer
after the roadsweeping-team
have driven to their depot
by the People's Palace.
A paper lantern
in an adjoining building
implodes softly
and without warning.
Nothing interrupts –
or is allowed to interrupt –
the sleep of officials.
Or their mistresses.

iv

The speeches of the camp's orphans
are learnt by heart.
They are timed to perfection
for their Nativity Play.
Pre-pubescent angels
descend to the audience
bearing the news
from Herod's country.
Later, if they're good,
there'll be a prize of jam
for the best ascension
made by a child under ten.

v

'What happened then?
Well, the Red Army
reached Voronezh.
They pitched camp
in the cemeteries.
Stakes were hammered
hammered night & day.
A din like a hunting party.
Their stakes in our green turf
 above my father & mother,
 above my gran & grandfather,
 above the bones of their
 parents, above a hive
 of rotting gypsies.
Oh yes, the mauve soil
 received their stakes.'

vi

'What do I know of
Voronezh? I have
said goodbye to the city,
 the cafés, the tired
meniscus of canals,
 the willows, the park
with its one stubborn
 revolting sundial,
the gypsy women
 who tramp in
on market day –
 stone complexions,
eyes giving away
 nothing but what
might clinch the sale
 of that ring, or their
baskets brimful
 of idiot finches.'

'Resistance?
When I cut through
behind the theatre
        of the University
I tell you, its walls
        drummed with speeches.
All day, they'd fretted
        over two items:
        'The downturn in steel
        dredging rods'
& 'the speedy order
for light weapons'.
The vice-chancellor hunched,
        shrugged (he'd rehearsed
the gesture). *We are*
finished. The army
is camped in our city.
We must arm ourselves
with what is to hand.
Look, like this.
He gestured, &'

'the sky was
pigmented with
smoke from fires
        in the cemetery.
The troops chopped
        wood, kept busy,
watchful. That's when
the mob attacked
(they were waiting
        for them with
machine-guns);
the city received
        its punishment.
& they passed on.'

'My eye was crossing
her face for an answer.
She back-tracked
       to when we "existed",
when she & I flung
open the big shutters
bigger than any book
       & the whole thing
was redeemable.

Yes, here was the world;
here, simultaneously,
the woman with her story
telling how that bullet
strayed from the riot,
spiderwebbed the window,
& vanished without a murmur
into her white
frictionless throat.'

The First Circle

A green woodpecker visits my unwalled garden
and begins its rounds. It hacks a slight, millimetering circle
in the lawn, then revolves as though squaring up

to a mathematical problem, one too large for one head,
maybe a problem of style even, to be left in the ground
like a marker of where the matter was left off.

When I left our home for the last time, my head
exploded – as though a rifle had gone off
in the middle distance (maybe he was hiding in our garden;

maybe you had let him know I was coming around).
I had trouble holding myself to the ground; what was up
was I was dead. And this was the first circle.

The woodpecker hammers and scratches the small round
space, I guess, mimicking the hit of rain on a garden:
the way seagulls flamenco on a football pitch's centre-circle

where the least of the action lets the grassblades off.
From the wear of the crimson secondary feathers on its head
the woodpecker is likely to be three years old. It flies up.

I worked up to leaving you over five years. I kept my head,
told you I loved you (and I could not not). I kept it up.
You strayed through our home while I – was underground

all that shift, mining for your grief, watching for that white circle
of air where this labour could stop, where you slip hands for the off
and go from under that ceaseless rain into this garden.

The woodpecker struts back after one hour to its cut circle
and waits for real rain. It seems this animal is all head
and strategy. It seems as patient as a small green general in that garden.

I want to shout, clap my hands, and make its little confidence blow up.
But, because the woodpecker has crafted a trap, like a death-trap on my
                                                                    ground,
because the catch is the beak's eye and art, then I hold off.

I take off my head. It is the same face you kissed as you sloped up
to our bedroom on that last night in our home. And how I ground
into you, knowing next night would be his. And how I was miles off.

Or how this grief is the age of that woodpecker in the garden,
a problem of style even or of timing for a predator in its circle.
Not you, waiting in the rain in your green coat, when I'd gone ahead

finally into this garden (I made your little confidence blow up).
But that this garden is the first circle; and here, love, is my head
to be left in the ground as a marker for where the matter was left off.

47

An Infinite Point

A ribbon bound to your finger, an aid for memory
to say three words, *maybe* and *maybe* and *maybe*.
How your conscience travelled the distance saying that.
But we got down to nerve, gut, love bite.

Take a dream sequence in which a whole cathedral
hardens to sheer crystal. Where spiders
abseil out of the sun, open you up like surgeons
and bind you again so very cleanly, cleanly.

It's the way with dreams. So with mathematics
two lines thrown to an infinite point
converge, finally, with what could be love.
Below it your conscience shivers in its hive.

I'm a half-tipped mirror taking some of you in.
Maybe half-a-cathedral, maybe half-a-spider,
that's how it is. Maybe, that's how it is.
Forgive me then for putting it this way.

'Read half of it back to me quietly, quietly.'

St Lucy's Day

'the year's midnight'

Snow wakes you. It flies outside your window.
Fine parallels follow the shuffling cars.
Some sky-god plucks the god-of-all-eiders.
An ice-man instructs the trees to play dead.
Fine parallels follow the shuffling cars.

The weather is a television with its aerial down.
An ice-man instructs the trees to play dead.
Ponds are trapdoors you drop to death through.
The weather is a television with its aerial down.
The angels are above you with CCTV.

Ponds are trapdoors you drop to death through.
Christmas is the madman in red on a snowplough.
The angels are above you with CCTV.
Fir-trees retreat like armies on the snowline.
Christmas is the madman in red on a snowplough.

Your best friends are drunk, adrift in duvets.
Fir-trees retreat like armies on the snowline.
You promise me the whole of white earth if I wake.
My best friends are drunk, adrift in duvets.
Then I walk into the eclipse of St Lucy's Day.

I promise you the whole of white earth if you wake.
Some sky-god will pluck the god-of-all-eiders.
When I walk into that eclipse of St Lucy's Day
snow will wake you.
It flies outside our window.

The conclusion to a scientific paper is the hardest to write. You present the principles, the relationships, the generalisations shown in your evidence. You must examine unsettled matters and relationships. Do not evade responsibility: you must discuss the implications of what you've done, as well as any uses in the world. Too often the significance of findings is not discussed or not discussed well. Either end with a short summary or nothing at all.

Where the world ceases to be the scene
of our personal hopes and wishes, where we face it
as free beings admiring, asking and observing,
there we enter the realm of art and science.

Albert Einstein, 1932

The concept of this text is that each piece of writing is a scientific paper of itself, a series of findings. The practices of writing science and poetry are, for me, a single discussion of perception carried out with the same eye and ear, and in the same laboratory of language.

'Clearing a Name'
Muck is a term for family or clan; *Gaujo* is the term used by Roma for non-Romani. As with taig (Catholic Irish) or gyp (traveller) the terms are pejorative but used freely in Romani conversation. The actions of the police in this poem take place during the search for IRA sympathisers and suspects during the Mainland Bombing Campaign of the mid-1970s. The story regarding my uncle's drowning is part of our family history, and its mythology.

'Σ'
Sigma: Σ is the mathematical symbol for the sum of all data.

'Two Haiku Pennants'
Einstein: The non-mathematician is seized by a mysterious shuddering when he hears of 'four-dimensional' things, by a feeling not unlike that awakened by thoughts of the occult. And yet there is no more commonplace statement than that the world in which we live is a four-dimensional space-time continuum. Space is a three-dimensional continuum. By this we mean that it is possible to describe the position of a point (at rest) by means of three numbers (co-ordinates) x, y, z, and that there is an indefinite number of points in the neighbourhood of this one, the position of which can be described by co-ordinates such as x1, y1, z1, which may be as near as we choose to the respective values of the co-ordinates x, y, z, of the first point. In virtue of the latter property we speak of a 'continuum', and owing to the fact that there are three co-ordinates we speak of it as being 'three-dimensional'. Similarly, the world of physical phenomena which was briefly called 'world' by Minkowski is naturally four-dimensional in the space-time sense. For it is composed of individual events, each of which is described by four numbers, namely, three space co-ordinates x, y, z, and a time co-ordinate, the time value t. The 'world' is in this sense also a continuum; for to every event there are as many 'neighbouring' events (realised or at least thinkable) as we care to choose. The equation $x'^2_1 + x'^2_2 + x'^2_3 = x^2_1 + x^2_2 + x^2_3$ is a complete idea which allowed Einstein to conceive Minkowski's 'world' as a four-dimensional Euclidean space, with an imaginary time co-ordinate.

Haiku: (Jap. 'amusement verse'): in recent Western practice haiku have a rigid quantity of syllables; but traditionally the form is a series of resonant pictograms presenting a complete idea or observation.

'Fulcum/Writing a World'
from William James *Reflex Action and Theism*

'An Infinite Point'
The final line and the spider-image are from a poem Osip Mandelshtam wrote in Voronezh on 15 March 1937. All other poems 'after Mandelshtam' take their bearings from one line, image or idea in the original poems. They are not translations, versions or 'imitations'.

Dedications

'Mathematics of Light' is for Charles Tomlinson; 'Two Temperatures for Snow' is for Michael Hulse; 'Two Haiku Pennants' is for Peter Blegvad; 'Ozymandias to You' is for Paul Muldoon; 'Intexti' is for Jane Stevenson; 'Redwings and Magnetism' is for Roy Fisher; 'The New Life' is for Jeremy Treglown; 'Simultaneity' is in memory of Allen Curnow; 'St Lucy's Day' is for Siobhàn Keenan.